PRAISE FOR *IT WASN'T EASY TO REACH YOU*

"Dan Meltz's poems are so intimate it almost feels like prying to read them. They're so funny and bold and moving though, that you can't help yourself."
  —**David Sedaris**, New York Times bestselling author

"Daniel Meltz sees with 'new eyes.' And few poets see so clearly the colors in the visible—and the invisible—spectrum of love, the pleasures and the pangs, the clarity and mystery. And few poets convey these colors in language more fresh. Here, under the covers, is a fluid taxonomy of love in a language with no expiration date. Follow the lines of these poems, their 'fallopian squiggles,' listen to the music of these poems, their 'intrinsic marimbas,' and you will be dazzled by the colors refracted in the prism of their words. Actual feeling is everywhere in these poems, feeling transcribed with unmatched passion and a fleet, witty, conversational—and dazzling—eloquence."
  —**Stephen Ackerman**, author of *Late Life*, winner of the 2020 Gerard Cable Book Award

"Daniel Meltz's beautiful first book, *It Wasn't Easy to Reach You*, is an absolute thrill to read. While the title seems on one level to be a joke about the book's long-awaitedness, it also slyly gestures toward the collection's underlying theme of human connection and the obstacles that need to be overcome to achieve it—like the 'booby-trapped frog pond' on the way to love, or the self's 'stubborn grandiosity peeping out of its/ shameful hiding.' We encounter many pleasures and surprises as we follow the speaker's circuitous search for the things that give meaningful connection to a life, which end up including kindness, friendship, love, and poetry itself. Meltz's voice, both playful and urgent, draws us in, and the poems have a liveliness and immediacy that somehow make them feel personal not only to the speaker but to each of us. Reading them is like finding a message in a bottle that traveled far in time and space but whose book-length note turns out to be addressed directly to you in the here and now. Believe me, you'll be glad it reached you."
  —**Jeffrey Harrison**, Guggenheim recipient and author of *The Names of Things: New & Selected Poems*

"Meltz's *It Wasn't Easy to Reach You* reached me easily with its original cast of thought about the everyday goofs and terrors of our lives and our relationships. He is approachable and surprisingly accomplished and he wields a sure grasp of what counts even when we're not certain exactly what it is. Daniel Meltz, poet, arrives in print like Athena, fully formed. And yes, his 'words got all over my shirt and pants.'"

—**Felice Picano**, Lambda Foundation Pioneer Award winning author of *The Lure* and *Like People in History*

"I swear you've been waiting for this book, waiting for a poet with Daniel Meltz's earnest exuberance, his witty and spiced intelligence, for those sly observations that make you say, YES!, for his word play and foreplay, his rhymes straight and slant, and for the honest emergencies and hard-earned serenities they record. Not just Frank O'Hara and Kenneth Koch and not just a bone-deep intimacy with life's most essential mysteries, these poems cohere as if the energetic delight of the art itself floated around everything. You'll wish he was your best friend, and the good news is, these poems will accompany you—and elevate your own thinking—as if he were. Daniel Meltz has worked wonders to reach us, and now we're his forever."

—**Jessica Greenbaum**, author of *Spilled and Gone* and *The Two Yvonnes*

"Buckle up reader, it's going to be a bumpy ride. These intelligent, clever, beyond the surface poems by Daniel Meltz will make you blush, laugh and nod your head in agreement. Like a present-day Frank O'Hara the poems in *It Wasn't East to Reach You* contain velocity and movement, both psychological, emotional, and intellectual. Meltz is a poet of urban wonderings and urbane wit. Here are the truisms of everyday life, from the 'funereal/monotony of the long lines at Capital One,' to the sudden revelatory realization of 'It wasn't a question of what/to remember, the diving birds told me, but who to forget.' These are grown up poems that pull no punches. And when I say grown-up, I mean from the perspective of someone who has allowed time to bring them to a place of full and gratifying expression."

—**Tina Schumann**, author of *Praising the Paradox* and winner of the Moon City Press poetry award for *Boneyard Heresies*

IT
WASN'T
EASY TO
REACH YOU

Poems
by
Daniel Meltz

ttt

First Edition.

Poetry
ISBN: 979-8-218-51324-5
Author Photo: Amy Dimun
Cover Photo: Daniel Meltz
Design: Jill McCabe Johnson

Published by Trail to Table Press, an imprint of Wandering Aengus Press.

Trail to Table Press seeks to publish literary works that transform our thinking about how we engage with the earth and each other.

Trail to Table Press
PO Box 334 Eastsound, WA 98245
Trailtotable.net

For Mike and Steven

CONTENTS

"You look for one thing and you find another."
—Muriel Spark

THE BALLAD OF TRASH AND MEAT

I looked all over for you, I was freaking.
I looked in every bar and every alley.
They said you'd just gone out or
you'd left a message for me, keep the faith,
or your car was in the parking lot, go see.
I went to the desk at the 17th precinct
and reported you missing.
They said it was too soon. I
went the next day and spoke to the
same sergeant, the one with the
muttonchops, and he said I was
too late. I looked for you in the *Post*
and the *News*, in the entertainment section.
I massaged my temples. I jaywalked.
I started smoking again. I dreamt about
Peter Graves (meaning I
wished you were dead). I ran down
stairwells. I leapt up escalators. I started
talking about how careful you were. How
careless you'd become. Mark Scheele (rhymes
with eely) noted how I was already using
the past tense about you. I met someone
new. My doctor. He was flirting. He
said Take everything off, though
I'd come about my heartburn. You know
me and doctors. Remember Dr. Fein and
his porno flicks in the dentist chair?
Anyway, what happened? I wondered.
And then it came to me. You were not
the Joe Wolf you said you were. You
were internal only, without any
margin of persuasion or remorse,
but I had loved you.

Narcoleptic Karaoke

I used to make lists of the names of my friends.
John, Larry, Ernest, Jeffrey, Mitch, Jean, Steve, Lee.
Then every couple of days I'd rewrite the list
on a scrap of paper or on a blank page in my diary.
Over time the list would change.
John, Sally, Jeffrey, Bob, Steve, Mitch, Amy, Bill.
Sometimes the list was lined up with my groceries.
Paul coffee John yogurt David shredded wheat Jeffrey tomato juice.
Or lined up with my groceries and the movies I'd seen.
Tom wheat germ A Room with a View
Amy chickpeas tuna Blue Velvet
I used to write down everything we talked about in therapy:
"'You're full of murderous rage!' 'I can't hear you!'
Then I burst into tears. She's right! She's right!"
As much verbatim as I could remember,
a one-act play three times a week.
I wrote down everything I saw and who I went with.
I recorded record highs and lows and the names of
the trees and the cocks I'd sucked. I recorded orgasms,
sick days, days I'd smoked pot, the length of the
movie, the number of hours since I'd last seen
Howie, since I'd first met Linwood, since
recorded rain had fallen. Inches of snow, days above
90, the 10 most populous, the driest, the loneliest,
the lone list, the one list, the on list, the off list.
Eventually I threw them out. Eventually you
wake up startled. What are you keeping lists for? What's
with all the legerdemain? It wasn't a question of what
to remember, the diving birds told me, but who to forget.

INTRINSIC MARIMBAS

I had 45 minutes so I went
to my favorite shoelace store on East
59th where the shoelace boy's always
flirting with the hot cashier in her skin-
tight top, they're appealing, although they don't
exactly take me in, and then it's out
into the street again where nobody's
sure if it's drizzling enough to haul out
the umbrella, the crowds are staggering,
the tourists in the glass Apple elevator, the arm-in-arm Brazilians, the
jaywalking bullies, the women in flip-
flops, toes serenely gripping, the man and
woman in gorgeous sweaters and matching
tans emerging from Bergdorf's, door held, two
big doormen with creased smiles and no sense of
pomp. I was here a couple months ago
at Doug's suggestion, it was drizzling then
too, he loves that little shoelace store, where
they also do shines and repairs, of course—
he was always saying "of course," which I
hated at first, it seemed so condescend-
ing, but then I came to understand his
odd expressions of delight. I do not
miss him but I miss the way he showed up
jumping and took off bouncing and looked at
me as if we were jackhammering sidewalk—worker and foreman, deep into sex.
But the crowds were exciting, the drama
of the crisscross, and then a walk
through Crate and Barrel, I bought a pillow, black and
green, two men helped me, one large one small, both
Filipino, a double-barreled cruise
that only added to the jolt of the
purchase, they put my pillow in a see-
through bag which made me a little embar-
rassed. I thought, let me take 58th back

west to get away from the people but
after a block I was bored, I wanted
to see the trees, so I circled around
and into the park where everything was
shockingly green from all the rain of this
week and the barks were black—greens and blacks as
exciting as the black and green of the
pillow I'd bought—the lindens in flower,
smelling like Juicy Fruit, soil, sopping,
mossy, quiet, the dark pain of quiet
so close to all the traffic, an awesome
Chartres with spandrel branches and stained-glass
leaves and fog in the spandrels, the fog's been
settled in among the building tops for
days, so unusual in midtown, you
can't see the top of Time-Warner, it
disappears into the fog along with
the top of the ugliest Trump in the
world and the memory of a boat ride
in the snow. Later, there he was, Doug, in
front of CVS, whispering my
name before he slipped inside.

I Will Go with Him I Love

1.
I sing the body electrocuted, flummoxed on the
pinochle table, double deck one life one death,
in the arms of a candid broad-backed farmer I
picked up on the Camden trolley, hooey this love
is fresh and exciting like a Fresca in a wounded
moon between a tuliptree and a deco cliff where
hawks are diving and thrushes flutter as the
hawks are whistling Get out of my way. I ping

the body of that hunk in Facilities, squatting in a corner,
drinking Jim Beam, talking to myself and the flat-
footed rhythms of your charm and habit like cymbals
and oolong kazoos in my head. I miss you aching on
the leather couch, the leather armchair, the leather
side chair. Wonton, meatballs, watered-down orange
juice, whatever you like. My fridge is wide open.
The curtains are screaming. The bridge is iced over.
You wore those shoes again, the black ones I bled on.

2.
Then I heard your voice behind my head. Then
I heard your voice on an MP3 player, string and
paste, heterogeneous hobo in time, melancholy
mojo, syncopated poppa, bopping down 6th,
with a flute, a potato and the magazine section
tented on your head. You said Give yourself credit
and Dream of sweet sleep because sleep is
where we meet and doubleverify forever.

THE ASHTRAY

I would like to put my brother in a home.
He'd be happier there with the bingo
and ham steaks. By brother I mean father.
There's a home in my area. An eyesore
on stilts. The receptionist is a middle-aged
blonde whose sister is a middle-aged
redhead who works for her on weekends.
One is like the other in a wig. Kind of
like my brother and my dad.

THE THERMODYNAMICS OF WALKING IN RHYTHM

Dad was a lush and Mom was a slattern.
The hitting and kissing established a pattern.
First came the rabbi, naked on a roof.
His aloofness was a front. His smacks were playful.
Then came Rick, sexy Little Caesar.
But his moods were awful.
He kicked and ran out.
While majoring in the arts
I started breaking hearts.
Then nameless he-men paid by the hour.
I was outraged and entranced by power.
Brief reprieve: in love with Steve.
But he never loved me back. Alack.
In time I met my Waterloo,
Frenchman Paul who liked girls too.
I stalked him once in a Gatsby hat
and caught him with Claire at the laundromat.
Then came John and our breathtaking fights!
And the thrill of all those slamming doors!
And Mark on his trembling townhouse veranda.
When he weighted me down and pressed me,
he depressed me.
It was hard to admit the hate that was in me.
And then I met you, a man of love,
loyal as a server room kept cold in La Jolla.
First crystallization the moment I saw you.
Second crystallization in a graveyard brawl,
two days crying and dancing in Montreal.
All those ready-made expressions:
- Our eyes met.
- The roof caved in.
- I've had it.
- I'm in it.
- I'll navigate you.
- No yes, you're right.
- No yes, no no.

It's simple, Michael.
We broke the cycle.

STILL LIFE WITH SISTER (ATLANTIC CITY)

I remember the embrace of an alcoholic
uncle—the benign smell of booze, like
aftershave. I remember the beauty of
a girl scout uniform, the gloves of
the cadets and the air of sororal belonging.
I remember the color TV upstairs, at
Aunt Molly Steinberg's, the first in the
building, 1961, and the splendor of the
NBC peacock. And I remember the
lady cowgirl downstairs, on the
black-and-white set, introducing cartoons
as the dinner smells started. I remember
the printshop of my nightmares and the
flood, my afternoon naps as Mom watched
Search for Tomorrow, and the night
of the hurricane, when we went from room
to room with a candelabra. I remember
being driven to my sister's school for
some reason, a block from the
Boardwalk. And I remember the boy named
Tim in my sister's class whom my sister
fell in love with. I remember the
masculine gym teacher, Miss Cutler, and
the students' reverence for her. I
remember dazzling Chris Carley jumping
right over his car door without opening
it and that he had on sandals without
socks and the top three buttons of his
shirt unbuttoned: he wasn't wearing
a T-shirt. There's a naked man in there,
I thought. I remember my sister's first-
grade play. She was the maid. My grandmother came over—the night before the
show!—to cut a newspaper freehand into
a pattern and make a costume, last
minute, incredible! including a frilly
white apron. She had also made the slip-

covers for our sofa, the design of which—
stylized vegetables in greens and black—I
can trace with my fingers to this day.
I remember the yellow record my sister
and I played over and over: *Barbie
You're Beautiful* sung by Ken. I remember
sitting in the tub with my sister, and my old
aunt Sarah (she was only, at the time,
52) reciting eenie meenie miney to determine
whose neck she'd scrub first. And I
remember how it all came apart when the
drunken uncle fell down the stairs, falling
and falling till the lobby landing, falling like
the man in the printshop dream.

MERCATOR'S PROJECTION

If you dump me
I'll drink till I pass out
and go to the theater the
next day hungover and
pissed. I'll get drunk
again that night and belt
out *8 Days a Week* at a
karaoke bar and bum a
cigarette afterward and smoke
it on the street. I'll keep
thinking I see you at the bar
and on the 6. The next
morning I'll stare at my hard-on in
bed and go to the theater again
hungover and pissed and then
eat eggplant parm and cookies for
dinner alone in my apartment
thinking the sweet glop'll help
me forget. But Monday I'll
remember that you hadn't
dumped me as much as I'd
projected every longing onto
you and you disliked it.

My Hand on Your Back Where the Pain Was

The pressure builds to come closer
like the impulse to love in a prankster
who tries to connect
when the signal is weak
and the reach back in time through the muddle of a week
that lapses into two weeks

wiggles around in the soul like
a weaponized Tinker Bell wand-ing among the ruins at
the end of the world
where cavepeople mingle with scientists
struggling to return to you
and squirt all over the bedspread.

At least it seemed that way
after three and a half days
when I was afraid to let you in again
because my soul as you know had collapsed
under the weight of your extemporaneous
song compositions and your hard knocks

on the original door—
swing it open into the glittering casino of
our love that took ten years of our
intermittent persistence to get to the point
of colossal payouts (despite minimal insight)
and still, still not enough talking.

Ten years and let's face it a little bit chintzy and
creaky in the morning but more often than not
with a razzle-dazzle orchestration
or just a guitar but either way with a tricky
syncopation and if you tack on those
extra three and a half days we're back to
our dopey divinity removed from any god.

Just Outside of Bowler City

my first teacher was my father
a sarcastic figure in underpants
he taught me how to
idolize and instigate
my mother
ran from him

she brushed her hair till it bounced
she used
the hairbrush as a weapon
she loved
the smell of the future
but she never stepped into it

my sister showed me her workbook
a multiplication table and
spelling lists
she read black beauty aloud to me
she turned on cartoons
heckle and jeckle
two angry crows

she told me about her teachers at school
the teacher with the swinging can
the teacher with the blubbery neck
the one with the
swishing stockings
the one with the
tangerine lipstick

we shared a bedroom with a kidnap window
we stage-whispered at daybreak
biting the cream out of cookies
we broke bobby pins in two
and scratched every inch of a crap credenza

OUTERBOROUGH CRYING JAG

Love built a nest in the flue
Tunnel of light from wood to sky
I was worried that what you said was true
I'd be better off with some other guy

The chimney made a blooping sound
Gurgling brick and a bird rushed out
Aimed for the ceiling then around and around
The cats ran in. You were too stunned to shout

Later when we talked on the grass
With the crickets in the redwood chips
You agreed with me that our worries would pass
Like the moon in retreat from a daylight eclipse

But what if your boys keep you hostage for years
And what if I never get over my fears
Though my faith in us you could say isn't stable
My faith in our love is a jumper cable

A LIFE GONE TO PIECES

I proclaim my woe at the podium of showoffs
in the voice of a clinker player piano
in the era of long distance
when mannequins were sadder
and there was never enough lube
in the love-machine crankcase

sweet smell of pigeon feather, beer and wet concrete
warming up a Rambler for a long ride to a lost kingdom
around a rotary of threat
among moviestar trailers and corktree caskets

how many poems was I expected to people
how many choruses of fire-roasted lamentation was
I destined to warble for the hypnotist
in the VFW parking lot

oh gray-and-pink eraser (gray for ink, pink for pencil)
that leaves its traces no matter how hard I rub:
abrade until the paper tatters

and all those buzzers of sleepless regret
Manny in the blackout
Ringo Starr

the fake cheer is getting to me
sunglasses everywhere, mascara, divorce

till other options proclaim themselves
in sunset purples and simple intransitives:
life is not an exacta bet
the dead-man's float is a magic trick
love is not a blister of desertion but a man

NINE LIVES

It's years since I've had an answering machine
but there are still many nights I turn
the key in the lock, eager to play
whatever messages were left
while I was working. At times I still think
the radio will go off when I turn
out the bathroom light though it's even
more years since that was how it functioned.
These are memories like dreams from
a previous life that flicker in an updraft
of mylar confetti at the back of the hero
waving from his jeep. We forget
how much we've changed, but the diarists
and the face-blind know. It's hard
for them to remember and recount their
humiliations on yellowing paper and in the
offended glares of the forgotten.

A Poem About Everything

Mostly all I want is what I'm used to. Like his picture lighting
the dark when my cellphone yodels. (The sunglasses shot.
Sending hoodoo up my back.) Or that moment when the message
PROBABLE SCAM shows up in the same blinding quadragon, a nightly
mystery sales pitch in Chinese. (Where in the world are they calling
from?) Life is change, yes, good, but minute by minute mostly it
isn't. It's the same six bazooka-proof friendships and their not
exactly platonic tingles, the same irritation of friendships of
obligation (two? two and a half?) and the familiar daily vanishing act
as I cede to the prerogative of whatever I'm reading, the funereal
monotony of the long lines at Capital One and the testing tents and
Trader Joe's, the elations of keychain library cards and stellar falafels
and easygoing orgasms and the truth sitting upright and shrieking
on a lunatic carousel of kangaroos and zebras. It's the pleasures of
pep pills and finally a quilting of measurable snow and the fingering
of elbow scabs and the knowing I'm right and the knowing
how long all along I've been wrong, how long is that, Steve?

But it's nothing like any of that, no not really, not after a while,
because the posters keep changing and the Tylenol's working and
the epiphanies mount and the worries recede like the flood at the
foot of Noah's volcanoes. I have dropped to my knees at the
altar of false enthusiasm and stood at the crossroads where the
GPS had no idea, but I climbed in quietly to the backseat of
whichever town car stopped to pick me up and it was him who
was patient there, him in the back, predictor of every possible
plot twist, Señor Casanova-Kowalski-Hamlet, minus the nail polish,
minus the melodrama, tosser of wisecracks and bocce balls knocking
other bocce balls out of the way enough to say You weren't really
paying attention, amigo. There were people who were nice to you.

COME ON OVER, THERE'S NOBODY HOME

I might step out of work, a job I loved, and onto the street and
sink into sadness, unfathomable sadness, as if the building, a structure
I loved, had rejected me and I would never be let back in.

And regardless of what the day had been like,
thrilling or miserable, studded with human connection
or dulled by dehumanizing drudgery, the same thing might
happen in the opposite direction,
after trudging out of the subway back in my neighborhood,
after death-marching through the crowds between the subway stop
        and my place,
6:30 or 7, rejected by the escalator, rejected by the MTA,
and then that moment of relief
as strong as a shot of tequila
when I'd get inside and shut the door and turn the lock.
Air-conditioned.
No longer assaulted.
Soundless and remote.
A shelf life of four to six hours.

The mother is the child of the daughter.
My dreams are a nautical sundial.
No standardized meantime in this zone without love.

BOSSA NOVA FOR PIANO AND RAM'S HORN

I had a dream last night and even
while I was dreaming it I knew I would
want to remember it forever
                              but I
forgot it, a pail of water overturned on a
boardwalk, not worth losing any more
sleep over, you on your side, me on mine.
A hint of prestidigital eternity.
A perfect life of unified slumbers amid the
banana fields of Ecuador
with one river flowing up and
one river flowing down. But perfection
doesn't mean much under these stainless
steel nostalgic skies throwing
lightning bolts down on the
chicken feed of our perpetual
anxiety, all those long-nosed masks hiding the
worried expressions of our indulgences
and longing, a distillation of every love
we lost. But then a wave
breaks, not of sea foam or mouthwash, but
of you and your waggles and your
all-encompassing he-man
hospitality like the mitzvahs of the tent dwellers
in the wilderness. May the Lord shine his
countenance upon you and by the
Lord I mean the DJ as you dance up
the aisle and leap to the stage and sing
I'm So Glad You Came by The Wanted,
as the boy from Ipanema puts a poppy in his hair
and cha-chas in the sand with Allen Ginsburg.

VARIATIONS ON A THEME BY SILVER CONVENTION

I was panning a lovesick video camera across West 57th Street, up
    that rise past the
bygone Playboy Theater and gothically sooty Carnegie Hall. I was
    busy immortalizing
wiglet meringues and patchwork jackets and salacious looks over
    Ari Onassis

sunglasses although the sky could not have been queasier, a sun-
    blocking butternut
tragedy color, as a garbage tornado sent a Milky Way wrapper and
    a *Daily News* with
a Mafia headline up toward the WALK/DONT WALK contraption. I
    was walking

without a purpose, ad-libbing a percussion to the syncopated
    whisper of corduroy
pants and the wham of the air around the boulevard Blutos who
    steamrollered past
me and the jangle of a carriage horse's agitated gag snaffle. I
    managed my progress

with *no body* to contain me, just the whir of the super 8 in my brain
    and the grace of
anonymity as I angled down Eighth, where *not one face* took a look
    at me, only
clouds pirouetting out of gutters and stovepipes as traffic played a
    rhythm on a

hundred-year-old manhole cover. Luckily I was tall already, even at
    age 14, so at least
I enjoyed the delusion of a presence. Though it wasn't until I moved
    in with Rick a
few years later—Rick X, who would become that public access
    porno

phenomenon—cantankerous, absurdly macho, down-with-the-
    government

Ricky—that I learned I had an actual body (it had something to do
     with his filthy
imagination and his stubby Crayola fingers) but then I forgot I had
     a body when he

dumped me at the Gilded Grape (only five months together; I never
     wanted it to
end) because I'd failed to seduce a sailor for a Valentine's threesome.
     I remembered I
had a body again in April 1980 when I danced and stripped and sold
     the same body

for a couple of weekends and the week in between. (Not as dismal as
     it sounds.) But
I regressed to the mean of misery after that, when I reconnected
     with Florindo of
the scissored jaw and back acne who did everything he could to
     crush my body.

(What exactly was it that I wanted him to crush? Why was it so
     gratifying to kvetch
about him?) Then at the Boy Bar a few months later I picked up
     Pierre—no
accident—he was lean and happy (I determined it would only take
     Just. This.

Much. To change Absolutely. Everything)—and we made love all
     night, no sleep
whatsoever, full strangers he and I (he came twice; I came three
     times), a magical
glow that still radiates off those pages in my diary to this day. I
     exodused from that

lovenest, however, lickety-split, like Moses out of Egypt (just
     matzah and water for
me; I'm serious) until a couple days later, back on 57th, after Pierre
     had kept calling
me, after he actually tracked me down at work and asked me what
     was wrong with

me that I didn't want to see him again, "I mean I could understand if you were
    if you were
incredibly *reesh* or incredibly handsome, but even *zen*," and like a
    moose in a
heatwave who never loses touch with its moose body I understood I
    was here in

New York, as here as the soot and the Solow building, and I knew
    where the insight
came from—from the literal hereness of my actual body—from
    Pierre's
participation in that actual body—and so I saw him again, maybe
    eleven times total,

because no, sadly, we never fell in love, but his challenge took root
    in me and became
my own portion and so to those who say There's Never Any
    Answer, There
Ain't No Answer, That's The Answer I say in all probability you
    gave up too soon.

SOMEWHERE MY LOVE

If he passes you in the hallway, snub him.

If he shows up in a dream and you don't understand why he's there with you in the middle of the night, passing you in the hallway, snubbing you like a petty middle manager, write the details down in a diary and set it on fire.

If he passes you on the street and says hello to you, pretend you're deaf.

If he sends you a letter after twenty-three years of gratuitous silence, send the letter back unopened.

If you happen to slit the letter open by accident and read it, in his ostentatious John Hancock handwriting, blaming you for all of his misery, put the letter away in a strong box.

If he's been living in the next apartment all along and he's never grown older, never gained weight, has in fact become more attractive and more successful, stumble onto him by accident, thinking you're knocking on the door of the super, and ask him about the lobby renovations.

If he's in slender pants and Jeff Goldblum glasses, as charming and incandescent as a Tinseltown record producer, and he welcomes you heartily, but a bit like he doesn't quite remember who you are, act absurdly pleased to see him again.

If you've prepared pointed phrases, even whole sentences, with a plan to destroy him, adopt a French accent to deliver your points in.

If you decide to tell him how delighted you are to be a Coney Island fortune teller, how much cozier your apartment is than his is, how much happier you are with your untroubled conscience and mischievous love life and credit score of eight-forty-seven, don't tell him till after you've fed him the poison.

If there are telephones ringing in the graveyard out the window, across American Chestnut Street, don't pick them up.

IT WASN'T EASY TO REACH YOU

I was coming at love from two directions,
from the direction of laughing attraction
and from a hard father. You see
people like this everywhere, in
just this pickle, faces open and
lusting, eager to do whatever
you tell them, anticipating the smack.

They attain to high position, they
play the numbers every morning and like
me they want to be bound to
you forever, lying together,
running my hands along your
body, where your father used
to touch and switch. Forever
and ever like the permanent
bronze of the wind in a
pair of statue pants.

MORE ABOUT LOVE

I got the message early on that love is
a risk and active which sounded like an
episode of *The Fugitive* so I wanted no
part of it although I went on dates like
the next guy and wrote poems after sex
about falling and fighting and rough
undressing. But you know it made no
sense, why I couldn't be in love or be
in love and not feel anxious every minute
about the fragile love's crumbling, this
when I thought of love as risk only, as
some kind of boobytrapped frog
pond—which it is—but if you stick with
it, like sticking with a stickshift (you stall
and stall until you finally feel the gears
give), then, maybe then, after hitting
and screaming, after feeling completely
stupid and crass for making demands and
forgetting to think, you're driving.

Hoopla Serene

You are majestic with a stoop and omnivorous.
At what velocity am I falling?
Humankind considers and remarks and reconsiders
the plush kiss, the plush ticking.
Can it shake, nap, render?
Is it friend or relative calling?
As sure as at the 11th hour of
November 11th the Armistice was signed, I will see
you tomorrow. I don't know Spanish
or the best generosity but I like
your smooth unbroken skin and your
smell and salt, the illusion
that you love me.

You are sitting on the sofa like a pasha.
I tear right into your harem pants.
Let's have a look, a lick, a rejoinder.
It's nothing people talk about during the workday
but it's the workaday subtext.
I remember telling Ellen about a colleague
and his girlfriend,
about how happy they seemed,
and her saying we had no way of knowing
as we didn't see what they did in bed.

You polish off a soda and a story—a rich illustration
        with an unexpected moral
and extemporize some more and growl, bemoan and moan,
you purr in the beigest armor,
conceal so much and few and sadly
with a soupçon of silly
and candy breath.
Let's have a look, a lick, oh honey,
you talk during sex like it isn't even happening.

Naples, Florida

A morning is six mornings here
In homes from blue to blue.
There are fewer than complications
In these sand forests
And doubling fronds.

That pink streak in the evening sky!
That shiny line that divides the sky!
And glows like a crack
In the black egg of heaven.

One young girl beside the lighted pools
Checking the time of her shy body
Does one lap and one lap
In recorded time.

LESTERVILLE

I will never again disappear for
you like a friendly vapor or a sad
wife Lester I'm a man and so are you.

We were walking in Chelsea last April 12th
during your first co-op panic when
you said how splendid I'd been! Disappeared

was what I heard. Like an Argentine
leftist: your braggadocio blew me off
the map. But I'm a man, I realize

now, as I step serenely out of the
pink convertible as large as my apartment.
I will never again disappear

for you or a literary agent or a colleague
or this weather that insists on thermal
meltdown or whatever. You are

less and less to me now Lester.
And here it is Friday! Your anxiety
day! I will never again be your
wife Lester. I'm a man and so are you.

CATACLYSMIC PATERNITY

There's the you at birth and the you that's taught and the you you
     concocted.
It's tricky to keep them separate.
All of them are you.

(It isn't tricky to keep them separate if you've titrated them to a
     roughly similar temperature.
Think Jane Goodall and James Baldwin.
Think Willa Cather and the greats of the baseball diamond.) (The
     ones who didn't drink.)

But here you are, drinking, trying to reconcile the three murky yous
as you settle into drink number three
and the stopper slides from the stem of the golden hydrogen balloon
that landed on your lawn
(mammary of lamé deflation)
which at first you thought was a stray crustacean
and then you thought was a UFO.

These are hints to the schizo reconciliation.
You're an alien and a crab and a gleaming surprise on a lawn.
You'll never really know how it got there,
wrinkling and softening, rubbery and depressed.
Grand opening? lawn party? fugitive from three states over sent to
     scare your inner bejesus?
But leave it for now.
Keep it that way.
Nothing bad happened.

STATISTICAL HIGH

I couldn't take it anymore. Thomas Cromwell,
Thomas Wolsey, Thomas Howard, Thomas More.
It was like all those frickin' Josés in *One Hundred
Years of Solitude.* So I put the Toms to bed (enough
is enough, Dame Hilary) and dreamt about Cissy
on the skids and wearing hot pants, the indefatigable
platinum blonde perched perilously on the Palisades,
as the wind blew through the rat fur and Shareen
booked a trip to Thailand (who can she fall in love
with there?) like Wendy Hiller in *I Know Where
I'm Going,* like Napoleon's brother in *Napoleon
Dynamite.* The Scrabble tiles were locked in place,
the ancient Egyptians were carving their jackals, the
paraffin lovers were making their way across the
drought-cracked Plains and a brassy bitch in stilettos
and Ray-Bans was barking into her cell on the
crosstown 8. It was an hour or two after leftover
wedding cake, I had an email from the newlyweds
(proof)—*"we're in Quincy now, touring the tombs"*—
an email from the invalid (poof), an email to the
recluse (oof), three days of cool between days as
hot as Hill City Kansas, Maureen and Nanette in
love (or not), paintings as rococo as Victorian
wallpaper, the Queen with her glasses on, reading a
statement, the jobless of Cyprus, the cats in the
sun, a slutty waiter, a buttered baguette, the Jolly
Rancher cherry and the apricot, the French,
I was here in these days for you and me both
but primarily for—you know—for you.

JANUARY 4, 1990

I was on my way to the library
        to pick up a book for Jonathan
which I thought was on reserve but wasn't,
        Confessions of a Mask by Yukio
Mishima, and all around me loomed the
        buildings with their lights on
in the falling fog and the hard urban
        blam of a hip-hop Chrysler and drill
and whistle and the whoosh of the traffic cop's
        cape-like raincoat, fifty or
so people coming right at me from
        fifty or so distinct directions,
the air is charged with them, the
        buildings stood in a bath,
a stone thunderbolt, a giant geranium,
        I am glad I live here, and I passed
and repassed the double information desk
        looking first for fiction then for poetry
and fiction again—THE DONNELL LIBRARY
        DOES NOT RESERVE FICTION—the
mood is modulated, like most libraries',
        it's across from the museum
where the mood too is modulated
        and it was packed on a Thursday evening,
people in trench coats and loose pants
        and loose silken hairdos,
I had three new library books, I had the
        music that makes me feel tall against
the tall tall buildings, ascending into the fog,
        reaching heaven finally, as they were intended to,
riding up the sides of the heads of insomniacs,
        I walked fast across the hexagons,
Tavern-on-the-Green trees dressed
        in Christmas-lightbulb dresses, the same
apartment ceiling corners repeated at the
        fifth-story level across the street, bookcases,
African statues, columns, canopies,

the intimacy of 6:30 lighting, I was
thinking about how I swallowed you whole,
there's an alien buttinsky inside
me who mooches off my pleasure,
I remembered how at one time the only
fun I had was walking like this around town
or riding in the back of a bus,
observing and oblivious, riding higher and
higher and quieter, a fuzzy rush of
no-home quiet until I reached
home, but that's all changed.
Even what hasn't. I entered Ellen's lobby.

Free Estimate

The first time you open the window
late February or early March and the
TV's off and the comfort of hallucinatory
warmth and quiet comes—it is actually so noisy!
the grinding teeth of a bus, a siren,
a truck, a sneeze, the ahhh of
the world as it breathes in and out like
a catnapping giantess whose respiration is
without interruption, her inhaling
indistinguishable from her exhaling—just
after Presidents' Day
at the end of a sooty clammy Tuesday
that dirties the milkshakes up and down
Broadway, a whiff so strong
of big fat impending and it isn't
spring either, spring's as far ahead as
May or as far behind as the previous
May, it's every known season plus a lick
of the dog that licked you: envelopes
with money, the thrill of an earth-
quake that does no damage, the day
it all kicks in after the pillow talk.
This is what excites me (you say), specifically
this! Please do it every chance you get.

Rabbi Stripped Naked

I
still think about him after all these years, the way he grabbed me
after class and pulled me
up to the roof, the way he cornered me
and smacked me,
his hairy arms in leather straps. I
can picture him under the locker room shower. I
can summon my overnight with him and his sexy wife. I
dream him. I
google him. I
remember his fallopian squiggles on the blackboard. I
remember his mishnah about a master and his slave. I
remember the rumors about his classroom nervous breakdown. I
think I'll write a book about him. I
drove past his apartment house in Teaneck. I
knew he couldn't possibly still live there. I
realized it was only an apartment house in Teaneck. With archaic
    crenellations. I
thought it was a perfect representation of him, a gorgeous fake
    castle he took me
to once. And it was there in his throne room that I
began to fall out of love with him as I
simultaneously fell for the student he'd so thoughtlessly invited
    along with me,
son of another rabbi.

POUGHKEEPSIE KEEPSAKE

The scattering sparrows, the scooters
scattering, the boss on a business trip,
the loss of hearing, the lost roots,
the last episode of *Lost*, the
missed opportunity for a thick steak
or a life on the stage, the death
of Norma Walker, the washed-out
bridge, the bridge.

The wind on the bridge, the view
up the winding Hudson from the bridge,
the vibrant fall colors, tangerine and
apricot and blood, our regular booth,
our regular waiter, oh sacred
heart, we love you.

Fennel, fennel seed, Manhattan, a
Manhattan cocktail, everyone ordering the same
drink, my life with you, your breath
in mine, back to front, toboggan,
to begin, to begin from Wednesday,
to email, text or call,
to wait like a waiter,
one tree blooming,
coming—arrived—or on the horizon.

LAST EDIT WAS SECONDS AGO

Used to be a bungee life off a rusted bridge on a paisley
river named a superfund site during the Nixon
administration. Used to be bouts of vertigo and
homewrecking and acid trips on the railroad tracks and
la-di-da books about Japanese dance and identity

swaps and shoplifting *The Bell Jar* at the Brentano's
in the Village that became a Duane Reade. Until I
tomahawked the bungee cord and sproinged like a rock
from an Oldenberg slingshot onto lower Second Av
where that notorious disco the Saint used to

be, marked by a grease stain in the shape of a gunned-
down body. Every part of me was busted but I still had
the high-pitched bizzbuzz of Yessir or Nosir against my
swollen intellect which echoed through a decommissioned
subway station where a corporal played *Taps* on a plastic

trumpet. If only I had the one word, be it strength or
emergency or anything as big and unmistakable as that
to snap me out of stupendous stupors, but as soon as the
word seemed to fit the situation it escaped through a
nostril so I discontinued talismanic buzzwords and realized

that if I wanted to stick around I'd have to get professional
help and return to the vocabulary at some point. That
some point is now. And though the word was changing
up until yesterday (words like connect and proportion and
father) the forever word is easy now, it's kindness.

OF A SPECIAL TYPE OF OBJECT CHOICE IN HASIDIC MALES

It was one sex always together and often they were naked
together, watching each other's bodies, keeping
each other's secrets. You would see
them fresh from the mikvah
with their

beards still wet and their eyes still red from lack of sleep or
mesmeric russified vodka hangovers or germs on the
surface of the ritual water. Every morning
in the Catskill swelter
Yussie

schooled us in torts and damages on the saturated grass. He
took to me. I took to him. I loved the summer-camp
Talmud lessons. All those wacky convolutions
about wine casks
blown

improbably off a roof and tallises discarded on the streets of
Babylonia and disorderly oxen and smart-ass slaves.
Yussie sat back in an Adirondack chair,
swing-dooring open
the cover of

his Talmud, leather-bound red, as big as an atlas by Encyclopedia
Britannica, with his still-wet beard and
his still-red eyes because even in
camp those guys took
dips every

morning in the mikvah. Yussie would get me drunk in the
dining hall most Friday nights on weed-killing rotgut,
a hundred-and-ninety proof (I was only
15), ostensibly
to toast

the Rebbe but also to let off youthful steam (he was 21; still
unmarried) and to rail against the forbidden marquees
that lit up 42nd Street (*Naked Came the Stranger,*
Mona the Virgin Nymph;
he knew

the titles exactly) and to clang me (youch!) on either side of
the yarmulke and fasten onto my buffalo ears and
smile at me like it's time for a
kiss. He wasn't simply
proselytizing.

Uneasy Listening

I never wanted to listen
because they never stopped

talking which was a way to
guarantee that I'd never be

seen as existing and what is it
with that endless yammering

anyway? So many people do it.
The words spool out in

ribbons of anxiety. They
sploosh all over the editing

console and shoot at you like
firehose water. If you try to

understand, you come up
with excuses like "Their

parents always tuned them
out" or "They're insecure

about the mark they make"
but still you're caught in the

line of fire and the words get
all over your shirt and pants.

Outstanding Performance by an Actor in a Supporting Role

She lights cigarettes from cigarettes and can never bundle warm
    enough. He has
Chevron stripes across both delts and a wiseguy smile. The
    daughter likes to
Squeeze the son with possessive headlocks. The grandmother likes
    to jab herself in
The rolled-down thigh as seagulls angle out the window, high
    overhead, in isopropyl

Martyrdom. She's as scrawny as a scallion but they call her Big
    Freida. There are
Children in the dirt and hiding under buildings. There are children
    in the evening till
The moon comes out. There are ice cream sellers in white with
    bowties pulling on
Silver sundown latches with a heartbroken suck on the seal. There's
    the squash of

Adjoining cardboard apartments on a dandelion corner near a
    supermarket where
Groceries roll out on conveyor belts. And the outdoor movie with
    its dialog wafting
Over a black steamy night, a plinking river. Romantic patter.
    Psychotic screaming.
The solution of a morning when there's nothing to adjust to. The
    solution of a

Teacher who is sexy with second graders but not in the way you
    think. The other
Teacher, the man teacher, who betrays them with his manly powers
    but who makes
Them want to relinquish their lives, anything to be with him, while
    somehow getting
Rid of his wife and kid. There's the night they know they love each
    other, Pete

And Noreen, at the Peppermint Lounge. And Gray, right after his
    father dies, alone
At that bar where the Samuel Beckett look-alikes go, punching out
    a stranger. And
Macaroni Bob with his elbow on a mantelpiece, eyes almost crossed
    with thoughts
Of his grand ambitions. Lost loves of exemplary character: a
    dynamo, a romeo, a

Harlequin, a conqueror. The languages they speak! The half-
    finished joints they
Pick up off the concrete floors after open-air concerts! The
    kaleidoscopic hard-ons!
The opportunities for self-pitying sobbing—thrilling neurotic
    interludes accompanied
By Rachmaninoff—and the disappointments too fresh to be
    understood. Oh

The guys you might follow around through the streets of the Far
    West Village like
A detective with only a courtroom artist's sketch to go on, brothers
    of the unrequited
Crushes that amount to a single archetypal crush—a lot of people
    are him—you
Know what that feels like, don't you? And the friends you can count
    on to get

Desperately trashed with and dance with or hug like dipsos in a
    cinnamon-tinted
Dipso movie, same friends since you first got started. Elizabeth
    Bishop, Eartha Kitt,
Henry James, Patricia Hitchcock. The widow who lives with her
    hard-ass mother
For 68 years in a mannish hat and coat like the hat and coat of the
    psychiatric matron

In *A Streetcar Named Desire.* The ecstasy dealer whose wife leaves
    him flat so he never
Bothers to love again and remarries a farina-white seamstress with
    dominatrix lipstick.
Plus of course his whimsical nephew. And you—you!—with your
    two-thousand thread-
Count palermos of love and nowhere else to go or hide because I'm
    futures in your history.

DEPARTMENT OF TUESDAY

I was safe in your arms.
Money was tight.
But there were no holes
in the elbows of my shirts.

We went to town.
We necked on a butte.
I was thrilled to be enthralled.

Ten days passed.
The exit lights blinked on and off.
The lust came ferocious and undecoded.
I wanted to fill my body

entirely with you.
The flowers arrived.
The paper came out.
Love descended fast

all the way down to the basement.
I was inspired.
Empty of all philosophy.
I was full of disapproval.

I couldn't sleep for weeks.
I cried out of happiness.
Your birthday stunned me.
It was 74 degrees and brilliantly

sunny on the deck of the pleasure cruiser.
Kids fished. Teens mooned us.
You walked ahead.
Memorial Day, Labor Day, Yom Kippur.

Sundays turned in the wind
like hanging paper. A kiss,
more thunder, a kiss, a bad party.
Two seats together in the very first row

looking up like fortunate babies
at the raving mommies.
A marvelous disappointment! I see now.
I wanted to fill my body

entirely with you.

GET OUT OF TOWN

A million motives
circle the square of his soul
like pigeons, alarmed
formations, falling
in circles, lifting like the
shy eyes of his childhood,
he's a hundred parts
scared of the love
that's offered. That's what Tom
says. (Hundreds of parts.)
He's trying to drive it out.
He's testing his freedom.
The three blurred glimpses
of the future, received
on the milky ball of the
air, show the pigeons
roosting on the eaves of
the cathedral, show them circling
endlessly over the square, show
them circling once
and dissolving like steam
to be rained down later.

LIKABLE BALALAIKA

I traveled the world on tiptoe
never fully landing on
sidewalk or poopdeck
a charming fellow who
wasn't quite with you
weightlessly waiting
on the gangplank or the
downbeat that determines
when the lights go out and
I can finally wear the
expression my face was
aching to spread across
magical midday walnut daydream
and a king-size margarita.

I was wrong about you.
I was wrong about your son.
I was wrong about the world
and my place in it. I was
wrong about the rule that
every wrong must be avenged.

On a Murphy Bed Mattress Full of Easter Egg Straw

I would write and the lines would spool out of me. It was a
physical need to keep defining myself but I never felt
defined. I filled notebooks. I covered walls. I hung a
pen around my neck. That was the strangest. The pen around my
neck. I counted out the beats of the words on my fingers. I broke
the thesaurus. I consulted the forms. Pyramids, houses, con-
certos, puptents. Anything to give a shape to my thoughts that ran
screaming from the feelings my thoughts churned up in
rampages of anxiety and unbroken hours of un-
considered scribble. When I had no money I scotch-
taped notebooks together and wrote poems and plays and
seriocomic novels starting from the back next to the
inside cover that in a store-bought version would show a
weights-and-measures table. When I had a little money I bought a
real notebook. When I had a little more I started watching TV.
It was while channel-surfing that I saw it all clearly. In the
groundless bravado of Wile E. Coyote. In Anne Bancroft's persistent
fingerspelling. In the pitiless debating of the whiners and the
chest beaters. On the faces of the chubby kids turning cartwheels in
the Disney promos. In the AIDS reports. In Mike Wallace's
wrinkles. In Barbra Streisand's tears. In the squalor after the
flood. In the hubris after the landslide. In a softened Archie
Bunker, in a confrontational Edith. In the wind in the trees.

I saw it. I took a picture of it. With my graduation camera. Mike's
face morphing into Barbra's. God's feet slipping into a
sinister pair of slingback Enna Jetticks. It's in the lines,
see. The lines that differentiate the heads from the curtains, the
ankles from the pantyhose, the other from the me.

All I Have

The night pressed in.
Humidity swelled the screens.
Crickets cheeped.
They sang of claustrophobia.
I threw aside pillows.
I wrestled the sheets.
I thought, That phonecall was short. He no longer loves me.
The radio mumbled.
A murder.
The heat.
I spun the dial.
"can't take it."
"Don't!"
"We toppled a record."
"Well I'm happy to be here. Ecstatic in fa"
I switched it off.
I started on one of those alphabet games I play in my head like
       counting sheep.
Movies or books with one-word titles.
I stopped at F. *Frankenstein.* What was the point?
I traipsed to the kitchen.
I turned on the tap.
Be honest with yourself, I thought.
I admitted I was glad for another empty day without you.
I admitted I was sad about the way things went.
I filled a glass and gulped down water.
I shook like a lighter that just won't light.
How had I wound up lathered away
to a sliver of soap?
Son of Mr. and Mrs. Perhaps.

FURTHERMORE, THERE'S NO REAL TELLING WHAT PROPELLED US HERE

Uber, tornado, romantic aspiration, deep psychological
insight, deep horniness, whatever it was; and whatever it
was we said to the other seventh-grade boys to get them
to pull their underpants down, and the fights we had with
our earliest boyfriends, the fights we had with our earliest
therapists, the epiphanies with our therapists, such as the
realization that we never liked Eddie, our best friend for
14 years! the true confessions of a mercenary nitpicker, the
trips by subway, bus and foot to a nude beach in Queens
where we first met Miguel and his friend who worked at
Stop and Shop, the irrational hangups, the telephone
hangups, the fixations on straight guys, storming out, giving
in, giving up, makeup sex, the razzmatazz of a half-open
shirt, the locker room at the Y near the tracks where
that French guy Adrian's pubic hair was as strikingly black as
Batman's boots, the tomboys of Totowa, the railroad
workers with the Winston packs tucked in the rolled-up
sleeves of their undershirts, the thud of the beat of Donna
Summer's *Spring Affair* as we entered Uncle Charlie's
South, East 38th Street, kings of the moment; and those
dark days as busboys where everyone flirted and the
waiters lived high on exorbitant tips and wore tight pants
and had sexual superpowers, the Howard Johnson's in
Times Square where we loafed between dances and joked
about the johns and read a little *Sweet Cheat Gone,* the
sneaking in for the second act, *Evita, Chicago, Equus, A
Chorus Line;* the one-night stand with that hotshot from
Charlie's with the stash of sticky Lebanese hash, the fried
potatoes at David's Pot Belly at 3 in the morning, the
realization at 3 in the afternoon that a hit from a low-
octane Needle Park roach and a *Mary Tyler Moore* rerun
were about as good as it would get in 1979, a plan to buy
a bus ticket to let's say New Orleans, a life-or-death
turning point, then waking up in a change of weather,
another night at a different Y, at an L in fact, an L-
shaped room, where the object was relationships

Hate Ache

You know you're angry if it makes
you angry that they call you angry.
You know you're less angry when the
imputations roll right off, make you
laugh in fact though there are still
residual and freshly harvested
anger tomatoes eager to be sliced.

Water Under the Bridge Over Troubled Water

The linoleum of the forest floor
is pebbled with bluestone tablespoons
that play to a rhythm of
hemlock-dappled inhalations.
Why don't we rest at the waterfall
and empty our pockets into the stream
that'll whirl away our miseries
toward the purple inking of the sun.
I was going to mention mosquito stings
but remembered to keep my big trap shut.

Again at the fire
the money's been counted,
the branches aren't scritching
at the shredded panorama,
so much of our lives has gone by
by now.
We were all the way up at the top
of that mountain, no trees to
interrupt the compass, and it was
easier then to understand where
religious people might get their
religion and the flashy people
might build their mansions
and the burning fields
we inevitably wade through, waving
our jackets to clear the smoke, might open up
to an amateur's camera
that like it or not recorded every
slight, every squabble, every kindness.

So don't stop reading. There's still lots of
time to rip it up and start again
knowing what you know. Maybe
you'll track your changes or cover
your tracks and assume a new persona
with all of its freedoms and
all of its pitfalls but maybe it's
best just to open your bag
and let security flash a penlight in
and wave you on.

SULTRY SILK TREE

we've been stupefied with sweat while big wilting corrugated heat
        boxes tumble out of the sunrise and lunchtime's

even worse so no one's really moving except to rinse out the
        airconditioner filter or cut up a cantaloupe

forget about the daily goals of 10,000 steps
today it's barely a hundred
no one's on the street
it's just as hot in the Catskills
and the cat is splayed out on the floor like a murdered acrobat

can't account for those meowless hours so might as well wash them
        down with
whatever beer has the highest alcohol content
though some of the evenings thereof are beautiful unexpectedly

glamorous gusts of potato breath out of the night as the sidewalks
        murmur

and forks and steak knives jingle on outdoor plates and rounds of
        laughter tumble up Columbus and the calm of the hundred-
        third day in a row without a jacket makes a person glad about
        everything

even those things the person isn't too sure about such as indoor
        plans and the specter of a violent death and the story of your
        advancing flirtation with the FedEx guy

AFTER THE HOLIDAY

How is it that I should so love my niece and so revile her taste in
        sofas
or adore Mike's brother Rich who's always bringing up *Twelve*
        O'Clock
High as the best movie ever or my therapist, even her, with her
        insights
and instincts that have reconditioned my very synapses,
        referencing all
of that lame sci-fi and in love with Sean Connery? And of course

Mike's no fan of *Citizen Kane* or *All About Eve* and
Julie has that grim preoccupation with Salvador Dalí
and Kelly goes for all of that unscripted fare and He Who
Stays Nameless likes to guzzle urine straight from the penis.

So is this another matter of the stalemate of
love or certain things in the end not mattering
or my stubborn grandiosity peeping out of its
shameful hiding? (I really thought I had
solved that problem once and for all.)

Meanwhile the dishes are done and the
leftovers packed and headed home with the
gratified guests and life is systematically streetlight-lit
under a skim-milk moon as the liberals and carolers
and redheaded freckled masters of the universe saunter
in the shadows spreading politics and pot breath and
come-what-may—make that come-what-December—in
the dwindling days of twenty-nineteen before the whole
world shakes and the sirens punch a hole in every nightmare.

BACK WHEN HOPE WAS FUN

It started after she fixed her bite and cut her hair, a layered cut but softer, more feminine, a blowout flip with Creamsicle highlights, and the old Hope dropped away, a shack in a sinkhole, no more hiding behind the Yoko hair and a mouth clamped shut. She threw back her head. She beamed. She threw back her head and worked on her tan. She walked into a room lit by a dozen disco balls like a model modeling this year's latest in personality reassignment surgery including a wise-ass warmth in the beaming and a whole new wardrobe not limited to purple prints of gigantic swooshes and boomerang blacks and a cleavage-proclaiming lamé cami. This period lasted three years.

It's not like life hadn't mattered beforehand. There was high school boyfriend one-eyed Jay (BB-gun accident; acrylic prosthesis) who introduced her to sandalwood cones and her womanly fire, surprisingly sweet-tempered Jay Lagattuta, with his mismatched suits and tickets to Birdland and business selling 'shrooms and hash without a piggy markup. He made her happy because they were matched in their losses and their persistent wishes to keep getting lost and their love of diners but if at times they were jolly they were afraid to be jubilant because of remorseless patchouli bad-luck jinxes as scary as capital punishment which were more than likely drug-induced.

Back when Hope was fun she had overcome every obstacle such as lackluster academics, a mother who didn't like her and a self-aggrandizing bartender father who started her off with nameless sensations of touchless unconcern. (Richard the Lizard Heart.) She made a decision (along with righting the overbite) to stop refusing dancing and noisy laughing and walking home and dating accountants and choosing a favorite and betting on a favorite and coquettishly nursing a brandy alexander at splendiferous Maxwell's Plum. Oh the glamor. Oh the cabrides.

She would wait on line for a movie without complaining. She would speak at length about coworkers and evil bosses and pause for as long as you needed, in turn, to tell her about your own toxic workplace. She would hunt down personalized birthday presents that made you feel loved—special and unique—a seven-color cardigan from Macy's, a kittenish poster for *Bell, Book and Candle…en français!* (*L'Adorable Voisine.*) She could tell you you were her best *best* friend and you knew it was the truth but then another truth confronted her, the mess of her wasteful suffering never completely unsuppressed and understood, and she gave way.

The gifts became leverage.
The glamor turned glacial.
Her boats took on water.
She scared away all her friends.

THREE STANZAS ABOUT HAIRCUTS AND OUR RELATIONSHIP

When the character gets a haircut, say Mia Farrow in *Rosemary's Baby* or Falconetti in *The Passion of Joan of Arc*, the audience lets its collective breath out. (Who knew there were so many bones in a human head?) Androgynies emerge like Michelangelos out of the marble. You can practically touch the lumps. Does this mean the plot'll start to go haywire? Whichever road we take in the fork is a question mark, Joan of Arc, because really we don't know anything. It is just as likely that the choice is as wrong as it's divinely inspired.

So. Okay. Let's check on the baby. Only the worst of humanity would sneer at a baby. This redounds to kids until they're three. Remember Jack at two in fact at Utopia Diner 1995? We were all having pancakes in a booth behind a sourpuss perusing the *Post.* Jack stood up on the red vinyl seat and turned around and chirped out a leprechaunic "Hi mister" to the tabloiding crabass, and the man put the paper down, took off his specs and busted out crying.

You will never know everything about me but because of the fortress you haven't built around you I will know you better. And I already know you enough to know that there are certain secrets you aren't meant to know, like how much I still don't trust myself. Regardless, you cut my hair today, yet another Covid contingency, shoving my head around like a joystick, like a battered Flintstone bowling ball. I love you up to and including the finale. *Climb Every Mountain. Try to Remember. See Me, Feel Me. Send in the Clowns.* I surrendered to your bumptious buzzer.

Good Reception

You stumble on epiphany
while probing traumatic memory
(was it actually traumatic enough?)
with its mealy lack of flavor but with
aspirations of fruited greatness.
You realize who you are

and the 24 wheels that got you here
a truck so fast down the Pennsylvania
Turnpike that it spread
new weather across the rolling
remains of the Delaware tribe.
You buy tickets to the ferris wheel

that turns in the plaza of your
consciousness, tickets you printed
on your home computer, a trip way
up above the utmost horizons
and it's clear to you, finally, your
fat lonely self, that's who you are.

A lucky break, a vintage whiskey, as
the metronome of sunset ribbons
into a commonplace infinity that
no one on this planet can relate to so
you reimagine every hope to the size
of a smartwatch with all its bars.

Scratch all that, whatever you rely on, all
the waiting around for the interloping
overlooker to remind you of the
moment you got so out of touch that you
couldn't reflect (on your forfeited
loan, on your unbecoming character)—

And when you saw you never needed
him to overlook, you overcame.

Visible Invisible

visible

You can appear and reappear as much as you want.
You can fight your way through or love your way over.
You can estimate the closest price without going over.
You can castigate the dermatologist for making you wait.
I have written you a letter. It's two-and-a-half pages.
There's a younger man at the mirror in it.
There's the story of San Francisco in it
and the tragic tale of Nina Simone.
There's a walk down Lex where all the coffee shops are still boarded up.
There's a complimentary closing. Yours truly.
I am leaning on you. It's good to be back.
Last Saturday I wasn't so sure, given your Saint Sebastian complex.
But I was recalled by a Toyota airbag back to reality.

invisible

The weasel doesn't get much love.
Not like the ermine she becomes in winter.
You'll never find her in the snow.
You'll never find me on Google Street View.
Gone into a dream, gone to the bank.
Evanesced into a 99-cent store.
An upvote from a slipshod magician who disappeared in
his slipshod act in Asbury Park and never came back.
It was as true of Rock Hudson as it was of Amanda.
They were hard-to-find people but they made people happy.
It was hard to come back from the edge
where the highway simply ended because it hadn't been completed.
The getaway limo screeched to a halt and left a long skid.
We rebuilt ourselves and the tide came in and knocked us all over.
There are two kinds of people, those who rebuild and those who don't.
It's not like none of us doesn't want a sandcastle.
I am still not sure where you are.
Sometimes you retreat in a flash like a mimosa panicle.
I return with the sun. I return to you.
It's like *Imitation of Life*, 1959, with Lana Turner and Juanita Moore.
What it means to be invisible. The destitution of that title!

Try *Invisible Man* by Ralph Ellison. Try *Ladder of Years* by Anne Tyler.
Try a floral collared pop-over shirtdress, 40 percent off at Ann Taylor.
My friend lost a friend for being too meek about the old friend's faults.
The friendship dwindled.
I tried strumming louder with a fingernail strum.
Acoustic was my ukulele. "Don't dwell on your faults,"
I sang to myself, "though they be numerous
as toad bugs in a bayou. Just focus on how thoroughly
superb you are in every way. And apologize only once."

LULA BOOHOOED IT

Our love began in a petri dish no
father or mother and the fertilized
form uncurled in a series of
laboratory mix-up clinics with views up a
boulevard lined with live oaks from
a window as big as a Motherwell on
the 22nd floor. Our love was born on
a dancefloor in Canada. Our love said
nothing, still doesn't talk much, stupid
but playful, leaning in against each
other like gourds on a porch with a
knocking sound and an echo that squishes.
Our love needed schooling, got a couple lousy
grades and is still behind the others,
is failing some of its subjects (math
and shop) but does decent in English
and geography and is still of course our
love.

ODE TO THE XES

Dave can't even listen to that voice with all
the tongue in it but I love it. It's a voice that
rings from the Truman era. A thick chummy
opera-going child-molesting baritone of bourbons
in the morning. Meanwhile X reports that her
husband kissed a stranger, a woman in a
bar, a drunken kiss. As X reports that
his ex was coldshouldering him at dinner Wednesday
claiming he was exhausted, bringing two
friends along on what X assumed
was a date. While X reports that he'd
really rather kill himself, X
himself out, and it's my fault if he does. And
X has started house hunting, dear
diary, without me. I am stung but I'm excited.
as excited as rangy nervous wreck X
must've been when she realized she could
blow her hairdresser in the closet off the shampoo
room. As excoriating as X surely was when
she went to my boss behind my
back and wondered how I had all this
time to put out a newsletter. As
excessive as that blue-eyed X who
wouldn't stop staring at my dick in the
gym today like a blinkered banker. As
polluted as X—and while we're at it X—were when
they fell off their chairs every night for a
decade after hours of patient tic-tac-toe.
Passions to rival a Pasternak.
Miseries worthy of miniseries.
Timeclocks etched in adobe, stopped.
Will X get the axe at the dawn of the
seventh layoff? Will X's face blow up
again, explode like a popcorn, and
rekindle her Quasimodo? Why
did she live in chaos and squalor for
forty-five years? And all those dogs with

floppy ears who Darwin said had
little to be alert about—this is where I
differ with Darwin, remembering "Eex,"
red setter of Paris. I thought the world
would end when I told you how much
I love my life and finally moved my
desk near the window, away from the
gasbags, where I wanted to be. But
no one blew a gasket. Everyone put a
hand out. Even you. Poor John thought people found his
broadsides delightful but they didn't. "They
just think you're an asshole," I said. Then
I walked into the park and enjoyed the
rest of May. Oh and by the way, X, go
ahead. Kill yourself. See if I care.

LETTER FROM AN UNKNOWN POET

I fell in love with a guy who didn't even know who I was,
every night a gaudy misery with the windows open on crickets
and creek. Forty-eight hours without any sleep. That's how it
goes when you're hypnotized in high school. A mad fascination.
But who controls the memory? What kind of love is that anyway?
Isn't unrequited love love in fact because when love is in fact
requited it heralds a similar moral assurance and the
optimistic crackle of cellophane ice on curbside water.

Now that we're more sensible and don't scrutinize every
love swab under a mutuality microscope or treat every day
like an LSD love trip where each moment is imbued with
the same degree of urgency, from the misfired kiss to the
unsponged countertop to the long-delayed but clarifying
IOU conversation, we still find ways to suffer, you with
your dreams of the Manson murders and me with my
canned corn, eaten over the sink. You crouch in the arena
with a lion, I panic in an elevator stopped between floors.
Which doesn't mean we should just stop talking.

Let me start over. I'm sorry for acting distant. I am trying
to maintain a separate identity (this week anyway) as I
grapple with the meaning of my last poem entitled "This
Is Why My Life Has No Meaning, You Fuck," which will
probably never be published but which comes from the
same emotional storehouse of a high-school hypnotism.

Lost and Found and Lost Again and Again

Sometimes it's better to have the upper hand and sometimes it's not and sometimes there are no hands to be had in the first place.

Sometimes someone is always apologizing or overdosing on Lexapro, full of what Gertrude Stein classified as "servant girl being."

Sometimes it's best to spread love like mulch though it nauseates firmer temperaments but in the long run inhibits crabgrass from spreading.

Sometimes it's best for the snarky to dominate so that the nicer learn to dish it back and polish a sense of independence that lurks within a dependent nature.

And the ones with no hands to speak of: Invite them over, they mingle so effortlessly, although they don't necessarily make good bosses, yet they're so perfect for

each other when they marry each other that, even if one of them dies, they will marry again because their love life never made them feel inadequate.

I cannot lie that I like it when your personality changes and you look at me with a dreamy curiosity as if to say Who is the real unknowable you that can make me feel guilty.

THIS MORNING AS THE VAPORS OF A NIGHTMARE EVANESCED
(DAY 56 OF THE PANDEMIC)

contained in an unplugged Schenectady icebox
Saranned in a bandana
of loose parchment paper
tattered wax
Billy the Kid
magenta eerie
neon flashing OPEN
neon flashing BANG-BANG
cell bars shadowing a topographical touch-specific groundplan of America
with insets for a skimpy Alaska and a broken Hawaii bracelet
here we are again
going again
lining up at the stolen table
looking into the littlest mirror
preparing for the parade
in the clothes we fell asleep in
remembering the early coy cancellations
and the unpleasant pleasure of a crowded 7th Avenue
pressing along the furniture of elbow and gymbag and waffles of eiderdown
like rub-on transfers of the Riddler and Pruneface
remembering the echoes in the overheated palace of
Old Masters and flat-eyed bubble-bellied Mary-and-Jesus icons
scrounging for a list of reliable one-liners to leaven the lull
at eleven after the coffee wears off
and the statistics settle in
shooting in the dark
your eyes wide in the dark
the eyes I like most
pointing toward the window that looks out over the trees
out toward the
rise in the neighborhood
with all the varieties of spring green and lime green
and tangerine green and Martian green
a hopeful azalea zigzag

everything visible in the dark
everything
against our free-and-easy hopelessness
as perfumed as a graveyard
with its improv of diggings and forbidden plastic flowers
synchronize your Novembers, people
repurpose the hypodermic to insinuate a tattoo
into the topmost layer of afterward
and tell the world that
despite what the boneheaded berserkians assert
the best way out
is to twizzle in the bang-bang.

Broken Monitor

I have always had this eagerness to go, to
leave the party or escape the restaurant or slip
away from the ceremony celebrating the
ancestral limestone monoliths in the fire circle.

      When is this sacrament over already?
           Please stop your jabbering, jesus.
You mean this movie's two hours and 47 minutes?
           Get me out of here.

Even with you after that Saturday
of
deeper cahoots expressed
in
kisses the saints must kiss
and
orgasms (one with words one without) as thrilling
as the transubstantiation of a jalopy into a
Cadillac, I left as soon as I could because you had seen
so much of what I sought to hide desperately
so I desperately fled
toward the
relief of a flatter interior as cheerless as
an Olympic
butterfly swimmer who's disappointed that he won.

I have always had this eagerness to go and come back and go
forever and never come back but it was different after the batteries
died in both your clocks and my therapist told me that the
doldrums cover the smirks and the smirks conceal the hurt so we
mixed the colors smirkless and knew each other better, adjusting
our paces and relaxing our resistance and remembering that the
lame clichés of *Call Me by Your Name* were a reflection of nothing!!
yet

YOU made the difference my rough-cut
romantic who can't say anything about love
but can *do everything* about love
and I could lie around
forever on the sectional sofa

of your abiding openness and
defiant mispronouncings but
who are you anyway until now
I didn't know
convenient vision shimmering
until the removal was removed.

ECSTASY IN HACKENSACK

Those guys are on the wrong train which happens here a lot, you begin to think it's a problem with the station announcements. And then those two too. Wrong way, fellas. You took the Pascack train, the conductor says, and there's a long stretch between here and Woodbridge where they can begin to correct their course, thinking about what else they could've done.

When I pulled out this notebook to write about you because I am so full of the feeling of you that it is spilling over into these words about you I was wondering how to approach you here and then I saw them all in the wrong direction full of worry and frustration but eager to get back to where they started to fuck it up so I started there.

Acknowledgments

American Poetry Review
        "Lesterville"

Assisi
        "Poughkeepsie Keepsake"

Best New Poets 2012
        "Intrinsic Marimbas" (reprinted from *upstreet*)

CCAR Journal
        "Rabbi Stripped Naked"

Columbia Review
        "Naples, Florida"

Curator
        "The Thermodynamics of Walking in Rhythm"

40 Ounce Bachelors
        "I Will Go With Him I Love"

Imitation Fruit
        "Free Estimate"

Impossible Archetype
        "A Life Gone to Pieces"

Kind of a Hurricane Press
        "Just Outside of Bowler City"

Lavender Review
        "Lula Boohooed It"

Mudfish
        "Hoopla Serene" and "More About Love"

New Orleans Saints+Sinners Anthology 2024
     "A Poem about Everything"
     "Broken Monitor"
     "Variations on a Theme by Silver Convention"

Noon
     "Hate Ache"

Plume
     "Cataclysmic Paternity"

Salamander
     "Furthermore, There's No Real Telling What Propelled
         Us Here"
     "Statistical High"

Talking Writing
     "Nine Lives"

Temenos
     "The Ashtray"

Tusculum Review
     "Department of Tuesday"

upstreet
     "The Ballad of Trash and Meat"
     "Intrinsic Marimbas"
     "It Wasn't Easy to Reach You"
     "Narcoleptic Karaoke"
     "Ode to the Xes"
     "Still Life with Sister (Atlantic City)"

GRATITUDE

In addition to the beloved dedicatees of this book…I am grateful to startling poet and forever friend Steve Ackerman who never stopped encouraging me, not since 1976, Jess Greenbaum who published so many of my poems in *upstreet* and who's always been the most readable poet in the universe, Jill McCabe Johnson and Tina Schumann for their support and smarts and for taking a chance on me, Jane Blank for her legal-eagle eye, Mary Bisbee-Beek for her PR scope, Kathleen Warnock for all those careening nights at KGB on East 4th Street, Professors David Shapiro and Kenneth Koch for their checkmarks in the margins, Amy Dimun for her spontaneous posings, and Alison Jarvis, Beth Farb, Bruce Austern, Dave Turnley, Gerard Cabrera, Greg Sanders, Jacki Marino, Jed Marcus, Jeff Klein, Jeffrey Jullich, Judy Katz, Lance Evans, Linda Appel, Marlene Rubens, Matthue Roth, Maya Turnley, Mitch Karig, Oren Rudavsky, Peggy Hickey, Peter Bingham, Rob Byrnes, Robert Konigsberg, Sally Deering, Serge Royter, Tom Ott, Toni Szilagi, Tony Lenti and of course Zabbo for never (apparently) falling asleep while I was reciting.

And again, Mike.

www.ingramcontent.com/pod-product-compliance
Lightning Source LLC
Chambersburg PA
CBHW040013100426
42574CB00085B/1232